Zeppelin Raid on Edinburgh & Leith

2/3 April 1916

HUGH HARKINS

Copyright © 2019 Hugh Harkins

All rights reserved.

ISBN: 1-903630-90-8
ISBN-13: 978-1-903630-90-7

Zeppelin Raid on Edinburgh & Leith
2/3 April 1916

© Hugh Harkins 2019

Centurion Publishing

United Kingdom

ISBN 10: 1-903630-90-8
ISBN 13: 978-1-903630-90-7

This volume first published in 2019

The Author is identified as the copyright holder of this work under sections 77 and 78 of the Copyright Designs and Patents Act 1988

Cover design © Centurion Publishing & KDP

Page layout, concept and design © Centurion Publishing

All rights reserved. No part of this publication may be reproduced, stored in a retrieval system, transmitted in any form, or by any means, electronic, mechanical or photocopied, recorded or otherwise, without the written permission of the publisher

This research paper has adopted the Harvard Manual of Style for referencing. It has, however, not always been possible to adopt a standard referencing format for some of the primary source documentation

CONTENTS

ABSTRACT vii

1 Zeppelin Raid on Edinburgh & Leith – 2/3 April 1916 1

2 Glossary 34

3 Bibliography 35

ABSTRACT

On the night of 2/3 April 1916, Scotland experienced her first ever air raid when German High Seas Fleet Zeppelin *L*.14 bombed the town of Leith and the City of Edinburgh on the South shore of the Forth Estuary. This report details the raids genesis – showing that it was not an isolated operation, but part of a far wider ranging German campaign that involved a number of other planned Zeppelin raids in the area of the Forth Estuary and the East coast of England – details the raid itself and its aftermath. The report shows that only a single Zeppelin operated over Scotland on the night of 2/3 April 1916 – disproving the claim that two such airships bombed targets in Scotland that night, a fallacy that has endured for more than 100 years after the event. The report also shows that defensive measures were instigated to try to intercept the Zeppelin on its inbound journey – by a RNAS fighter aircraft – and on the outbound journey – by warships of the Royal Navy 2nd Light Cruiser Squadron and attendant Destroyers. This was the first recorded incidence of a fighter aircraft being launched to counter an air raid on Scotland, a historical fact that has gone un-acknowledged during the ensuing 103 years.

The report draws on documentary evidence from several archives held in a number of depositories. The major documentary evidence is taken from the Leith and Edinburgh Police Constabularies, the Edinburgh Fire Brigade, the Lothian Health Services Archives, German mission reports, British Admiralty reports on the airship raids and naval operations to counter the raid and a number of government documents/letters and personal circumstance letters.

1

ZEPPELIN RAID ON EDINBURGH & LEITH – 2/3 APRIL 1916

On the night of 2/3 April 1916, Scotland suffered her first air raid – a new type of warfare that would be developed throughout the twentieth century. This form of warfare was able to affect civilian populations some distance from the battlefields that were the scenes of the clash of armies. In regard to the British Isles, the U-boat blockade had a far greater economic and military effect on the nation's war effort than air raids.[1] That said, the Zeppelin air raids were able to instill a sense of vulnerability and apprehension in the population that was absent as an effect of the economic blockade conducted by the U-boat.[2] Only the German naval bombardments of British East coast towns/garrisons could rival the Zeppelin raids for their psychological effect on the British populace.[3]

Airships of the German High Seas Fleet would receive orders to attack the South, central or the North of Britain. The term south generally referred to the region of the Thames Estuary, the tem central generally referred to the Humber and the term north generally referred to the Firth of Forth. The major effort was intended to hamper naval operations emanating from these East coast estuaries through attacks on ports, naval bases, industrial areas and ships. Which areas were targeted depended largely on the wind (speeds and direction), the attacking Zeppelin force wishing to have the wind pushing against its course on the outbound journey to the target in order that it was a tail wind on the homebound journey, which would aid the airships withdrawal, particularly if the Zeppelin had been damaged or had suffered

---

[1] U-boat (undersea boat) was the name applied to German submarines that waged war against British commerce

[2] The term Zeppelin was applied to German airships in reference to Count Ferdinand Zeppelin, whom had developed airships in Germany, the first such craft being flown in 1900. Zeppelins were accepted for service with the German Military in 1909

[3] There were a number of major bombardments of British East coast towns and their military garrisons involving Battle Cruisers of the German High Seas Fleet from December 1914 to 1916

mechanical problems (Scheer, 1920). Such was the impact that weather could have on the Zeppelins flight that all too often they were unable to make it to the intended targets through being blown off their course, often by hundreds of miles, by high winds (Scheer, 1920 & UK NA).

Figure 1. This image depicts a military airship, LZ 77, showing the typical two gondola layout. This airship was employed on a raid over Eastern England in 1915. It was destroyed when it was shot down by anti-aircraft artillery fire when operating over the area of Revigny, France, on 21 February 1916.

The first Zeppelin raid on Great Britain had taken place on 15 January 1915. This raid was unable to reach the Humber region, its primary target, and instead dropped its bombs on Great Yarmouth and Kings Lynn, quite some distance to the East. The last Zeppelin raid on Britain took place on 5 August 1918 (Scheer, 1920 & NA).

Typically a Zeppelin (a lighter than air machine with a steel girder and an envelope filled with hydrogen gas cells) of the L.50 type was powered by five motors, each of 260 hp, which drove four propellers (the rear two motors were coupled to drive a single propeller. This provisioned for a maximum speed of around 110 km/h, depending on certain variables, such as weather conditions – the L.70 type would later be able to operate at around 130 km/h (Scheer, 1920). The L.50 type envelope had a capacity of 55,000 cubic meters and beam was 23.9 m. The airship gondolas, positioned underneath the envelope, were linked by a 196.5 m gangway through the envelope. Zeppelins of the L.50 type had a crew of 21 persons and carried incendiary bombs weighing 11.4 kg and high explosive bombs with weight classes of 50, 100 and 300 kg – bomb load was typically in the range of 2000 kg, consisting of several tens of small projectiles, carried in a mix of high explosive and incendiary warheads. Despite the low speed, in 1915 and 1916, the Zeppelin appeared able to operate over Britain with relative impunity, its high number of bombs – several tens – allowing it to attack multiple targets, often over a considerable time period. The low power of the early fighter/interceptor aircraft meant that they were often easily out climbed by the Zeppelin and, even if the altitude to attack the Zeppelin was reached (this could be around 3000-4000 m), this could take a considerable amount of time, by which time the Zeppelin had bombed the target and was outbound heading for home. Fighter aircraft were also hampered by the fact that Zeppelins were bombing in the hours of darkness making them hard to locate for the pilots whom were also hampered by the risks of take-off and landing during the hours of darkness, this often leading to the loss of the aircraft in accidents.

Figure 2. The Zeppelins in service with the German High Seas Fleet were primarily tasked with supporting the warships of that fleet, with various allotted tasks, including scouting and attacks on naval bases, ports and costal targets.

The subject of German air raids on Britain being conducted with relative impunity was raised in the House of Lords on 17 February 1916. Lord Oranmore and Browne raised the point with the government that 'Zeppelin airships raid this country [United Kingdom] and return to Germany with impunity' and questioned the government on whether or not 'it was contemplated to make such improvements in our [British] methods of offence and defence as will give greater security against such raids' (Hansard, 1916). Lord Oranmore and Browne followed his question 'what has been done and is being done with regard to the building of aeroplanes… powerful machines which could give rise into the air to fight the Zeppelins over this country?' with an impassioned speech that suggested inaction on provisioning defensive measures by 'members of the other House' [Commons] was due to 'many members of the other House' belonging 'to that school of thought which is called the "anti-gasbag school", whom the noble Lord considered were 'of the opinion that because up to the present [February 1916]' such raids had 'resulted only in the slaughter of a certain number of civilians, of women and children, and have done us no military harm, these aircraft are not worth the cost of their construction and the expense of training crews to man them' (Hansard, 1916). He continued

'I think no one in this House [Lords] believes that the German Zeppelins came here [Britain] merely for the purpose of murder… their chief object in raiding these shores is to do us military harm by the destruction of arsenals, barracks, munitions factories and other military works and though they have not yet succeeded in doing so there is no reason for saying that they will not be more fortunate from their point of view in the future. Every time the Zeppelins come they seem to be holder [probably should read bolder]. They go further afield… therefore they give us serious cause for uneasiness' (Hansard, 1916).

There was much truth in this impassioned statement as initial standing orders for Zeppelin attacks on Britain were for attacks to be mounted against 'military works, such as arsenals, docks, batteries [gun positions]…' and other military associated targets (Scheer, 1920). However, the difficulties in finding such targets inevitably led to non-military targets being struck (Scheer, 1920). The Fact that the Zeppelin raids were not intended as a purely indiscriminate bombing campaign is borne out by the fact that Zeppelins often returned with their bomb loads due to inability to locate a target – an indiscriminate campaign would dictate disposal of bombs over any part of British territory before returning home.

Figure 3. This photograph shows two women surveying damage caused by Zeppelin bombing, Edwin Place, Porter Street, Hull, in 1916. Such raids caused public disquiet as they appeared to be conducted at little cost to Germany. AIR 1

By the time of the armistice of 11 November 1918, the German naval Zeppelin force had lost 17 of its airships through enemy action on operations (Scheer, 1920), a loss rate of just under thirty percent. A further 28 were lost to other causes, such as 'stranding' during operations, or being destroyed in their sheds during air attacks (Scheer, 1920), extending the loss rate to just under seventy four percent. Such a high loss rate could only be accepted for operations that it was hoped could materially affect the outcome of the war, rather than as a purely terror campaign against the populace of Germany's enemies. In reality, the Zeppelin raids, and naval bombardments of British coastal facilities, could also be considered a way of bringing the war to Britain's shores, as part of the German attempts to force Britain to enter into peace talks, bringing the other allied powers with them.

Figure 4. Often erroneously stated as a target for the Zeppelin raid on 2/3 April 1916, the Forth Bridge was not a stated target of the German operation. The small sizes and destructive power of the bombs dropped by the Zeppelins would have had a negligible effect on the structure of the bridge. This image shows the 4th Destroyer Division and the Light Battle Cruisers HMS *Courageous* and HMS *Glorious* passing under the central arch of the Forth Bridge, circa 1917-18.

Evidence from the German and British archives show that the raid on the Forth Estuary that took place on the night of 2/3 April 1916 was only one of several such raids planned for spring 1916. While only a single Zeppelin would drop its bomb load on targets in the region of the Forth Estuary, no less than ten such sorties were launched or planned, only *L.14* making it to the Forth area on that fateful night in April 1916.

The first air attack on Rosyth naval base/dockyard, which is situated on the North shore of the Forth Estuary, ~1.5 km westward from the North end of the Forth Bridge, was planned for the early hours of 5 March 2016. This mission was part of an overall program of more assertive and wider ranging actions by the German High Seas Fleet to counter British light naval forces that were operating in waters close to Germany's North Sea coast (Report by Captain Schulze of *L.11* & Scheer, 1920) – such light forces emanating from British east coast naval bases and ports, including Rosyth. The report by the Commander of *L.11*, Captain Victor

Schulze[4] details that three Zeppelins, *L*.11, *L*.13 and *L*.14 were ordered to ascend commencing 12.00 hours on the afternoon of 4 March 1916.[5] As the three Zeppelins proceeded toward Rosyth, weather conditions, 'an ever-increasing strong north-north-west wind, bringing heavy snow and hailstorms', proved to be unfavourable to continue toward such a northerly target as Rosyth (Report by Captain Schulze of *L*.11 & Scheer, 1920). Subsequently the Zeppelin force abandoned the attempt to reach the primary target and instead opted to proceed to attack arms factories in Middlesbrough. *L*.11 eventually found herself near Hull and the commander reports observing *L*.14 drop bombs on or near that town and, after loitering for an hour or so to await the chance of clearings in clouds that had thickened, dropped her bombs in the vicinity of Hull to induce action by searchlights to allow better location of preferred targets – the harbor and docks.[6] *L*.11 then dropped more bombs on what the commander identified as such targets and then proceeded to aim for the fortifications at Immingham before encountering engine problems, compelling the decision to withdraw to base (Report by Captain Schulze of *L*.11 & Scheer, 1920).

The Zeppelin Raid on Leith and Edinburgh on the night of 2/3 April 1916 cannot be viewed as a stand-alone incident, but rather part of a wider operation conducted by the Zeppelin force of the German High Seas Fleet over the course of six days – 31 March-5 April 1916 – which covered the period just before, during and just after the New Moon, taking advantage of the increased darkness (NSM XV).[7] The Zeppelin raids themselves were part of a wider High Seas Fleet operation, with considerable elements of that fleet sailing in support. The two major roles for the surface warships was to recover crews of Zeppelin's that may come down in the sea and to intercept elements of the Royal Navy surface fleets sailing to intercept the Zeppelins on their return journey across the North Sea following their raids.

The first Zeppelin raid of this attack phase was launched on 31 March 1916. This would be a considerable effort involving the use of seven Zeppelins – *L*.9, *L*.11, *L*.13, *L*.14, *L*.15, *L*.16 and *L*.22 – tasked to attack London. According to NSM VX[8] two Zeppelins, *L*.9 and *L*.11 suffered mechanical problems and returned to base. However, the *L*.11 commander report on the raid and Admiral Scheer's report, dated 1920, clearly state that *L*.11 crossed the English coast South of the river Tyne and, after encountering anti-aircraft fire and wind problems as it attempted to bomb the docks on the Tyne, set course for Sunderland, which was bombed before *L*.11

---

[4] Schulze later died on operations

[5] This information corresponds to that held in British records, NSM VX, 1926 & Signals 1200, 1210, 1212 of 5 March 1916, held in I.D.H.S records

[6] NSM XV, 1926 concurs that both *L*.11 and *L*.14 bombed targets in Hull. *L*.13, after moving westward, then southward, bombed villages located in Rutlandshire and the Isle of Sheppey (Air Raids & Reports by Director of Air Services, H.S. 218

[7] The New Moon rose on the night of 2/3 April 1916, the night of the raid on Edinburgh and Leith

[8] NSM XV, 1926

withdrew and returned home (*L.*11 commander report, 1916 & Scheer, 1920). Information from British archives state that *L.*13 bombed Lowestoft where she was damaged by anti-aircraft fire and forced to return to base, dropping the remaining bombs, intended to be released over London, on what was thought to be Lowestoft, but was in fact villages located around 20 mile or so to the southward. *L.*14 bombed what she thought was central London, in the region of Tower Bridge, but was in fact a pier and oil storage tanks at Thames Haven (Airship Raids 1916).[9] *L.*14 then made her return to base. *L.*16 bombed Bury St Edmonds among other areas, damaging several tens of houses. *L.*22 suffered mechanical problems, which slowed her journey to the target area. She abandoned the attempt to bomb London as her delayed arrival would be conducted in the face of a fully alert air defence. She opted to coast to the Humber where the town of Cleethorpes was bombed, buildings being damaged and 29 British soldiers were killed with 53 injured when their billet was hit by a bomb. On her return journey she was engaged by gunfire from a paddle steamer in the Humber, but escaped unscathed and returned to base (NSM XV, 1926).

Figure 5. Zeppelin *L.*15, commanded by Commander Breithaupt, partially submerged in the Thames Estuary after being brought down on 1 April 1916.

*L.*15 dropped bombs on Ipswich and Colchester as she tried to find London, encountering anti-aircraft fire from batteries on the Thames coast, west of Gravesend. She dropped her bombs in the area of Rainham 'opposite Erith', Kent, and, around this time, was damaged by anti-aircraft gunfire (NSM XV, 1926). She set off for home on a north-east and then eastward course, being engaged by an aircraft during this phase of the mission – she survived the aircraft attempt to destroy the Zeppelin by bombs and explosive darts, but her buoyancy was gone and she came down in the Thames Estuary at around 12.15 am on the morning of 1 April (NSM XV, 1926).

---

[9] Thames Haven was located more than 50 km to the East of Tower Bridge

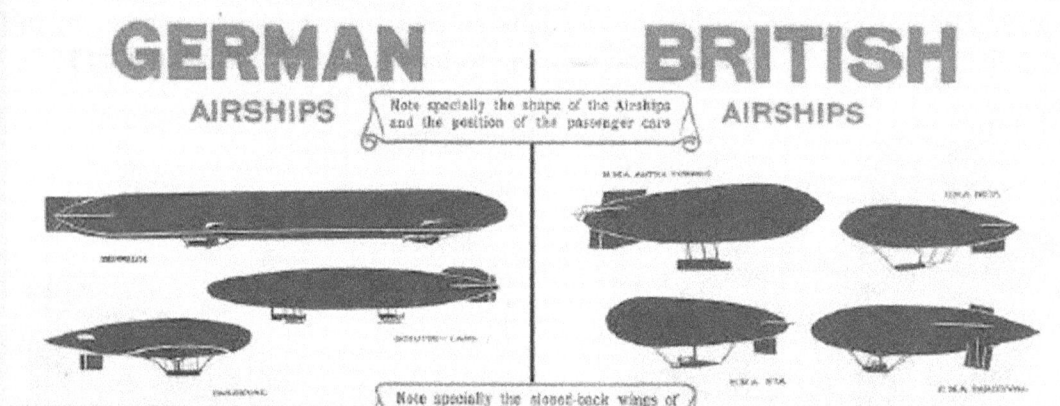

Figure 6. Part of a British Government air raid warning poster dating to 1915. Such posters were issued as a public advice service following the first air raids on the British mainland, which caused widespread concern and fear among the population, which had hitherto been immune to direct military action when Britain was at war in some distant part of the world. The main purposes of the poster was to provide information, including a small measure of identification of German and British airship/aircraft silhouettes, in order to reduce the number of false alarms, which could cause panic among the populace. The poster also advised what to do in the event of an air raid and its aftermath. MEPO 2/1621 (1915).

The raid launched on 1 April 1916 involved Zeppelins *L.11* and *L.17*. The latter airship suffered mechanical failure en-route to the Humber on the East coast of England, turning for home just short of that region, having ditched her bombs in the North Sea in order to lighten the ship and increase safety on the return and berthing (NSM XV, 1926). *L.11* crossed the North Sea toward the Humber, being engaged by gunfire from a Royal Navy Trawler patrol in the area of the Dogger Bank.[10] The airship made landfall on the English coast, to the South of the Tyne around 23.00 hours on the night of 1 April. She crossed over the towns of Sunderland and

[10] The Dogger Bank is an area of shoals, located in the North Sea some 97 km off the north-east coast of England

Middlesbrough, both of which were bombed in turn before *L.*11 crossed over the coast and proceeded across the North Sea. While the damage caused by *L.*11's bombs dropped on Middlesbrough was slight, consisting of little more than broken glass in a number of buildings, the material and human cost for Sunderland was considerably higher – *L.*11's bombs dropped on this town caused the destruction of around 20 dwelling houses with 22 civilian fatalities (NSM XV, 1926).

Sometime around noon on 2 April 1916, another Zeppelin raid on the British East coast was launched, the target being the naval base at Rosyth in the Firth of Forth, Scotland.[11] This time four High Seas Fleet Zeppelins were involved, *L.*13, *L.*14, *L.*16 and *L.*22 (NSM XV, 1926). Three German surface Flotillas were ordered to patrol and area from Horn Reefs to the northern part of the Dogger Bank. These forces hoped to intercept British light naval forces that may be dispatched to intercept Zeppelins returning from raids – the raid the previous night was clear warning to the Admiralty that Zeppelin raids on the East coast were a distinct possibility on the night of the 2nd and into the early hours of the 3 April.

Figure 7. The Destroyer HMS *Tristram* (Pennant number F 89) anchored off Rosyth, with the Forth Bridge in the background, circa 1917. It was Rosyth rather than the bridge that was the primary target for the Zeppelin mission to the Forth Estuary. WO

In a mirror of the previous night, one of the Zeppelins, *L.*13, developed mechanical problems and was forced to return to base, leaving the remaining three to continue their journey across the North Sea to the British East coast. Weather conditions were less than favourable, particularly in the western area of the North Sea where a northerly wind was prevalent. This wind pushed against the airships with the result that the general trend was for the airships to be forced southward, contrary

---

[11] It is stated in official British naval papers that the target was Rosyth and the Forth Bridge, but the later would have been a poor target for the types of bombs that were employed and too precise a target for bombing other than by a chance hit. The most logical conclusion is that the target was dockyard buildings at Rosyth, as borne out by German records

to the direction they needed to attain the objective. Abandoning any hope of reaching Rosyth, *L.22* crossed the English East coast and dropped her bombs over an area the crew thought was Tyneside. *L.22*, however, was much further North than the captain had thought, the river Tweed having been mistaken for the River Tyne. The Zeppelin bombed a factory, but although she retained the bulk of her bombs, thick cloud obscured the view of the surface forcing the Zeppelin to cut short her mission and return across the North Sea to her base (NSM XV, 1926).

Like *L.22*, *L.16* had abandoned the primary objective, Rosyth, due to being pushed southward by high winds. The Tyne district was selected as a secondary target area and *L.16* crossed the English coast around 23.00 hours on the night of 2 April. She dropped her bomb load some 19 km from Newcastle, with little in the way of damage being reported on the ground (NSM XV, 1926).

The remaining Zeppelin, *L.14*, which was commanded by Lieutenant-Commander Bocker, had been more fortunate in her crossing of the North Sea and was able to continue on-course for the primary target, Rosyth.[12] That said, the journey across the North Sea was not without incident. When off St Abbs Head, to the South of the Firth of Forth, *L.14* encountered a Royal Navy Destroyer patrol, which engaged her with ships guns.[13] She was able to continue on her journey, but was slowed considerably as the wind direction was now south-west, contrary to her optimum needs (NSM XV, 1926).

At 19.00 hours on the evening of 2 April, the British Admiralty telephoned the post office to pass a message on to the Edinburgh City Police informing them that an air raid on the city or its vicinity was possible due to the detection of the approach of one or more Zeppelins. This was done in accordance with a pre-arranged procedure in such an eventuality (NRS HH31/21). At 21.05 hours the military authorities issued an order for the civilian authorities in Edinburgh to put in effect air raid precautions, this order also being issued to other urban centres. On receipt of military authorities instructions, an order was issued to the 'Electric Light Department' to 'lower all lights' and the Edinburgh City lighting was lowered at 21.30 hours, this being the signal for civilians to take what anti-air raid measures they were capable of, such as turning off gas – lowering the lights was also the signal for road traffic to refrain from all but the most necessary journey (NRS HH31/21). Other civilian departments and organisations, such as the Central Fire Station and the Red Cross, were alerted to the potentiality of an air raid and all available off duty Police – Regular and Special Force – were ordered to duty (NRS HH31/21).

Although the defences against air attack for the targets actually bombed – Edinburgh and Leith – were very poor, there were a number of countermeasure

---

[12] It is pointed out in the official British Naval Staff History that Bocker had visited Edinburgh and Leith on a number of occasions pre-war in his capacity as the captain of a 'Hamburg-Amerika' liner (NSM XV, 1926). Such visits would have been of no value on the 2/3 April mission flying over a darkened area almost bereft of opportunities to take even a moderately accurate positional fix

[13] St Abbs Head is located about 40 or so km South East of the mouth of the Forth Estuary

operations put into effect to counter the Zeppelin on its inbound and outbound journey's. The Royal Navy Destroyer patrol that had engaged *L.14* off St. Abbs Head had forward a position report. The Admiralty forwarded a report to the Naval Air Station at East Fortune, located in North Berwick, around 30 km or so from Edinburgh, with orders to send an aircraft – Avro 504C – up in an attempt to effect an interception of the Zeppelin. Construction of East Fortune airfield, which would cover the Forth Estuary and Edinburgh, had been authorised by the Admiralty for use by the RNAS (Royal Naval Air Service) in September 1915. The main function of the base was to be for the stationing of airships for sea lane patrols in commerce protection and general reconnaissance, but fixed wing aircraft were also allocated, the first, a pair of Sopwith two-seat scout biplanes and a Farman arriving in September 1915. These would be joined by Royal Aircraft Factory BE.2c and the Avro 504C (National Museums Scotland).[14]

The Avro 504C was a single-seat development of the two-seat Avro 504, with a fuel tank occupying the position of the front cockpit associated with the 504B. The 504C was developed for RNAS service long-endurance (up to eight hours in the air) anti-Zeppelin patrols from British East Coast airfields, ranging from South East England up to East Fortune in Eastern Scotland. It was hoped to intercept the Zeppelins out at sea before they crossed the coast and were able to bomb their targets. The 504C was powered by a single 80 hp. Gnome engine and had a typical maximum take-off weight in the region of 419 kg, although this varied. Speed was ~130-132 km/h. Generally such aircraft could not climb as fast as a Zeppelin as was demonstrated operationally when an Avro 504B attempted to intercept Zeppelin LZ.38 during the small hours of 17 May 1915 only to be out-climbed by the German airship. The Avro 504B was armed with small bombs and explosive darts that would be dropped on a Zeppelin from above, requiring the intercepting aircraft to climb above the flight altitude of the German airship. The single-seat Avro 504C, eighty of which were built for anti-Zeppelin operations, had a fixed armament of a single Lewis machine gun, which could be fired upwards, through a gap in the upper wing section, at an angle of 45°, allowing it to attack the underside of a Zeppelins, thus removing the need to climb above the airship (BAE SYSTEMS Heritage).

A single Avro 504C, piloted by a Flight Lieutenant Cox, took-off from the airfield at East Fortune at 21.40 hours on the evening of 2 April 1916, with the intention of intercepting the approaching Zeppelin before it reach its target area. Following a fruitless search for the German airship in the darkened skies of night, the Avro 504C returned to East Fortune airfield, but crashed on landing, causing serious injury to the pilot (National Museums Scotland).

---

[14] The first airships did not arrive at East Fortune until 31 August 1916, almost five months after the Zeppelin raid on Edinburgh and Leith, East Fortune having been officially inaugurated as a RNAS station on 23 August 1916

Figure 8. Initially the two-seat Avro 504B was employed on anti-Zeppelin operations. This aircraft design, which was armed with light bombs and explosive darts, was unsuitable for the task of intercepting Zeppelins. BAE SYSTEMS Heritage

Figure 9. The Avro 504C was more suitable than the Avro 504B for fighting Zeppelins as it was armed with an upward firing Lewis Machine gun, negating the laborious and often impossible task of having to climb above the Zeppelin to engage it with the aircraft armament.

Prior information received by the Admiralty had allowed the formulation of an idea of the possible routes that could be taken by the Zeppelins approaching the Northumberland coast of North East England and the East coast of Scotland. To counter the expected Zeppelin raid on the Forth Estuary, Admiral Jellicoe, commander of the British Grand Fleet, ordered the 2nd Light Cruiser Squadron, accompanied by four Destroyers, to sail from Rosyth in order to position these forces below the flight tracks estimated for a Zeppelins returning across the North

Sea following attacks on the Forth Estuary and or Newcastle (NSM XV, 1926 & Jellicoe, 1919).[15] The Light Cruisers and Destroyers departed Rosyth around 22.00 hours on the night of 2 April 1916 and set course for position on meridian 1° E, between 54° and 55° W, where they patrolled through the early hours of the morning of 3 April (NSM XV, 1926).

Figure 10. The Light Cruiser HMS *Southampton* of the 2nd Light Cruiser Squadron, circa 1916.

Despite the problem presented by the high winds in the attempt to reach Rosyth, sometime around 23.00 hours on 2 April, the crew of *L*.14 observed lights emanating from the Leith and Edinburgh directions, enabling a navigational fix to be made, albeit, briefly, as the lights were soon lost. Without the lights for guidance the airship continued on its way as the crew attempted to locate Rosyth, slightly North West of Edinburgh and Leith. Rosyth proving elusive in the darkness, it was decided to attack the docks and harbor facilities in Leith-Edinburgh to the South East of Rosyth.[16] The bombs were dropped over several areas, most falling in the South

---

[15] In early 1916, the 2nd Light Cruiser Squadron consisted of the Light Cruisers HMS *Southampton* (Commodore Goodenough), HMS *Birmingham*, HMS *Nottingham* and HMS *Dublin*

[16] Edinburgh lays on the South bank of the Forth Estuary about 6 km or so South East of Rosyth. Leith is just North of Edinburgh on the South coast of the Forth Estuary

region of Edinburgh (NSM XV, 1926). Initially the British Admiralty reported that 13 people were killed and 'half a dozen dwelling houses' were 'wrecked' (NSH XV, 1926). The same document also states that there was no military objective for the Zeppelin to attack. This statement seems at odds with the report itself, which accepts that the primary objective was the Rosyth dockyards and that the secondary targets were docks and harbor facilities at Edinburgh and Leith – the bombing actually being intended to strike such targets. The inaccuracy of bombing from a Zeppelin inordinately reduced the chances of the intended targets being hit in all but perfect conditions, much to the detriment of the civil population, which all too often bore the brunt of such attacks.

Figure 11. Zeppelin *L.*13 was of the same type as *L.*14, which bombed Edinburgh and Leith on the night of 2/3 April 1916. *L.*13 was tasked to attack Rosyth on the night of 5 April 2016, but was forced to abandon the attempt to reach the Firth of Forth due to mechanical problems.

During the raid twenty bombs fell on Leith (NRS HH31/21/8 fols.11-17) with a further twenty four falling on Edinburgh ((NRS HH31/21/8 fols. 27-49).[17] As well as an accurate count of the numbers of bombs dropped, we can, with confidence, detail the types of bombs dropped on Leith and Edinburgh, as well as detail the damage and casualties caused by the bombing raid. This is possible due to the

---

[17] This includes a single bomb that landed in the water of the Firth of Forth at Edinburgh Dock, Leith

existence of a number of documents held in several archives. The major documents come from the Leith and Edinburgh Police Constabularies, the Edinburgh Fire Brigade and the Lothian Health Services archives.

BOMBING & DAMAGE AT LEITH – The Leith Police Constabulary produced a report on the bombing raid in response to a government letter, No 25478FA/2, dated 10 April 1916, which requested that such a report be compiled. The subsequent report, dated 12 April 1916, was prepared at the Chief Constables office in Leith Town Hall (NRS HH31/21/8 fols.11-17).

Including the bomb that fell in the water at Edinburgh Dock, Leith, twenty bombs were dropped on Leith – twelve incendiary and eight high explosive (NRS HH31/21/8 fols.11-17). Around 23.25 hours on the night of 2 April, a Zeppelin was reported to be over the Firth of Forth to the West of Inchkeith Island.[18] The direction of travel was reported to be Southwesterly, which took it in the direction of the Docks at Leith. From making landfall around Edinburgh Dock, Leith, *L.14* appears to have followed a flight path that was initially southwesterly, before heading on to a more pronounced southwesterly course, bombing the Albert Dock area along the way. The first bomb (1), a high explosive projectile, was dropped as *L.14* passed over Edinburgh Dock. This bomb landed in the water at the western end of the dock with the effect that two rowing boats were sunk. Two Danish flagged merchant vessels were nearby, these suffering minor damage in the shape of broken windows in the skylights (NRS HH31/21/8 fols.11-17).

The second and third bombs dropped from *L.14* were incendiary devices. The first of these (2) landed on the quayside at Albert Dock, but caused no notable damage as the incendiary was quickly extinguished by Police and other persons on the ground. The second of these incendiary bombs, the third bomb overall, (3) impacted in a yard area near Albert Dock. Although the bomb set fire to a wooden fence, no notable damage resulted as the fire was extinguished by Police and other persons on the ground (NRS HH31/21/8 fols.11-17).

(4) The fourth bombed dropped was a high explosive device, which landed on a grain warehouse located at Timber Bush. The roof was damaged and the flat located on the top floor suffered damage to parts of its wall structure. The explosion resulted in chunks of masonry being propelled onto properties adjoined to the warehouse, these suffering various degrees of damage described as considerable in the Police report, which went on to state the actual level of damage was not known at the time the report was compiled (NRS HH31/21/8 fols.11-17).

(5) The fifth bombed recorded (high explosive) burst on the edge of the harbor quayside, 'damaging the quay wall near to the Customs House' and also causing significant window breakage in dwelling houses, shops and offices nearby (NRS HH31/21/8 fols.11-17).

(6) Bomb number six (high explosive) landed on the roof of a tenement building, specifically 2 Commercial Street, several hundred metres South of Albert Dock. Part

---
[18] Inchkeith Island lays in the Firth of Forth, 6.7 km northeastward of Leith

of the roof was destroyed, as was at least one wall in the top flat where the first fatality was recorded – 66 year old Robert Love being killed when a shrapnel fragment from the explosion hit him as he lay in bed (NRS HH31/21/8 fols.11-17).

(7) The seventh bomb (incendiary device) crashed through the roof of a dwelling at 14 Commercial Street. The bomb carried on through an upper floor room, through the floor and the dwelling below, where it ignited. The room in the upper level house that the bomb travelled through was occupied by an elderly lady whom apparently rose from her bed and then poured water through the hole in the floor and extinguished the fire that had started in the house below (NRS HH31/21/8 fols.11-17). There was no reported casualties caused by this bomb.

(8) The eighth bomb (incendiary device) landed on the roof of a tenement building, 45 Sandport Street, to the South of Commercial Street. This bomb started a fire, which was quickly extinguished by the residents of the building. The only notable damage reported was that caused by the bomb crashing through the roof of the building, which was described as 'slight' (NRS HH31/21/8 fols.11-17). Two more bombs landed on Sandport Street (incendiary devices), the first of which (9) landed on the 'footway' of 9 Sandport Street and the other (10) landed in the 'yard at 9 Sandport Street', neither bomb causing any notable damage (NRS HH31/21/8 fols.11-17).

(11) The eleventh bomb (high explosive) landed on the roof structure of a building occupied by – Innes & Grieve, wholesale spirit merchants. The building was destroyed by a fire started by the exploding bomb, resulting in loss of spirits stocks estimated to have a value of £44,000. A number of shops and dwellings in the vicinity suffered shattered windows from the blast of the bomb (NRS HH31/21/8 fols.11-17).

(12) The twelfth bomb (incendiary device) landed on a tenement building, smashing through the roof of 15 Church Street and carrying on through the floor of No.15 and the ceiling of the house below. Both dwellings suffered significant fire damage before the blaze was extinguished. Although there were three residents at home in the upper dwelling and seven in the lower dwelling, no casualties were reported from this bomb (NRS HH31/21/8 fols.11-17).

(13) The thirteenth bomb (an incendiary device) smashed through the roof of the manse (church residential house) at St Thomas's church, located in Mill Lane. The bomb ignited and started a fire, which more or less destroyed the dwelling. All of the occupants, listed as the 'minister, his wife and servant' whom were all in bed at the time, escaped without injury (NRS HH31/21/8 fols.11-17).

(14, 15 & 16) The next three bombs (all incendiary devices) landed at various points on Mill Lane – a gravel area at front of Leith Hospital (14), the play yard area of St Thomas school (15) and the ship building yard of Hawthorn & Cos. (16) (NRS HH31/21/8 fols.11-17).

(17) The seventeenth bomb (high explosive) landed in a garden area of 200 Bonnington Road with no notable damage reported. (18) The eighteenth bomb (high explosive) landed in a courtyard at 200 Bonnington Road with far more costly effect. A one year old child was killed in bed by shrapnel that entered the room through the window. The notable material damage caused by this bomb was significant breakage

of windows and damage to doors (NRS HH31/21/8 fols.11-17).

(19) The nineteenth bombs, a high explosive device, landed on a railway line in the area of Bonnington Tannery. This device failed to explode. (20) The twentieth, and last, bomb to fall on Leith during the raid was a high explosive device that penetrated through the roof of Bonnington Tannery and entered a tank, used in the leather manufacturing process, before bursting. The explosion caused damage to other tank contents (NRS HH31/21/8 fols.11-17).

Figure 12. This map indicates, in black dots, some of the area where bombs fell during the Zeppelin raid on Leith and Edinburgh on 2/3 April 1916. Edinburgh City Archives

BOMBING & DAMAGE AT EDINBURGH – The bombs dropped on Edinburgh are numbered 1 to 24, but overall the 1st bomb dropped on the city was the 21st bomb that was dropped from *L.*14 during the raid on the night of 2/3 April 1916. The listing of 1-24 is not necessarily the exact order that the bombs were dropped. The first reports of exploding bombs coming from the direction of Leith were recorded at 23.50 hours on the night of 2 April. This is the time recorded for the first bomb to fall on the City of Edinburgh, bombing continuing intermittently until the last reported explosion at 00.25 hours on the morning of 3 April (NRS HH31/21/8 fols. 27-49). In this first bombing raid on Edinburgh, 24 bombs were dropped – 6 incendiary and 18 high explosive.

(1) The first bomb released from *L.*14 over the City of Edinburgh was a high explosive device, which, as noted above, exploded at 11.50 pm on the night of 2

April 1916. This bomb did not result in any casualties and caused very little material damage other than window breakage in streets as it fell on what was described as 'vacant… ground at Bellevue Terrace', which was located in the North eastern part of Edinburgh (NRS HH31/21/8 fols. 27-49). The blast shattered the front and rear windows of around 20 dwellings in Bellevue Terrace and most of the windows of the dwellings in tenements 48 and 58 in Rodney Street. In most, but not all cases, the window frames were significantly damaged and there was damage to the ceiling of a communal stairway at number 48. Other than dwellings, the windows of nine shops in Rodney Street were blown out, as were 30 windows at Canonmills School and six windows at Neil's Printing Works. In Heriothill Terrace the windows of twenty one tenement dwellings were blown out, as were the windows of five tenement dwellings, five front door houses and seven windows in Bellevue Parish Church. Windows were broken in a shop, two tenement dwellings and a single house in Cornwallis Place and in dwellings in a tenement in Summer Place. Close to the bomb impact site a small building of corrugated iron construction, used by the 'City of Edinburgh Fortress Engineers', was damaged (NRS HH31/21/8 fols. 27-49).

Figure 13. This photograph shows bomb damage to buildings in Lauriston Place that were located close to the Royal Infirmary Hospital. P-PL1-E-208

The course of the raid appears to have followed a path of direction close to the 180° South from the where the first bomb was released, as the second bomb (2), an incendiary device, landed on a road 'in the Mound' some 400 yards or so from Edinburgh Castle – there was no notable damage reported ((NRS HH31/21/8 fols. 27-49). (3) The third bomb (high explosive) penetrated through the roof of a house, 39 Lauriston Place. Damage consisted of a smashed roof at 39 and 41 Lauriston Place (adjoining house) and serious damage to the inner ceilings and dividing wall. The bomb blast blew out windows in a number of properties in Lauriston Place and nearby Archibald Place. There were no casualties among the occupants, but a fragment of the exploding bomb injured a man whom was in the street some 80 yards away. This man subsequently died from the injury sustained (NRS HH31/21/8 fols. 27-49).

(4) The fourth bomb (high explosive) impacted within the grounds of George Watson's College. The impact point was a mere 150 yards or so South of the impact point of the third bomb at 39 Lauriston Place (NRS HH31/21/8 fols. 27-49), indicating a continued southward trajectory for the Zeppelin course at that time. The bomb blast caused damage to stonework's on the steps where it fell. There was also considerable window breakage at George Watson's College and the rear windows of houses located in Chalmers Street and some windows in the Royal Infirmary Hospital were blown out (NRS HH31/21/8 fols. 27-49).

(5) An incendiary bomb fell in an area known as the Meadows, this is assumed to be the fifth bomb dropped on Edinburgh. No damage or casualties were reported (HH31/21/8 fols. 27-49). (6) The sixth bomb (high explosive) landed on a tenement block, 82 Marchament (Marchmont) Crescent. Following the explosion, recorded at 23.55 pm, a significant part of the bomb structure carried on through the floor of number 82 and continued through three more flats before coming to rest on the floor of the ground floor dwelling, 80 Marchament (Marchmont) Crescent. The roof of number 82 was destroyed, the floors and ceilings of the four dwellings that the bomb penetrated through were destroyed and there was significant damage to some vertical wall structures. There were no reported casualties from this bomb explosion (NRS HH31/21/8 fols. 27-49).

(7) The seventh bomb (high explosive) landed on 183 Causewayside, a tenement block with five single room and double room dwellings. All five dwellings were seriously damaged and an adjoining wall collapsed. The damage to this building was so significant that it was deemed a danger to enter at the time the air raid damage report was compiled. The bomb blast caused injuries to six persons (NRS HH31/21/8 fols. 27-49).

(8) The eighth bomb (incendiary) landed in the garden of a villa, 31 Hatton Place, with no notable damage reported. (9) The ninth bomb (incendiary) landed in a garden located at the rear of a villa at 28 Blacket Place, with no notable damage reported. (10) The tenth bomb (incendiary) landed in the grounds of the Royal Infirmary Hospital with no notable damage reported other than minor impact damage (NRS HH31/21/8 fols. 27-49).

Figure 14. Incendiary bomb, dropped from Zeppelin *L*.14, in the grounds of the Royal Infirmary Hospital, Edinburgh. P-PL1-E-021

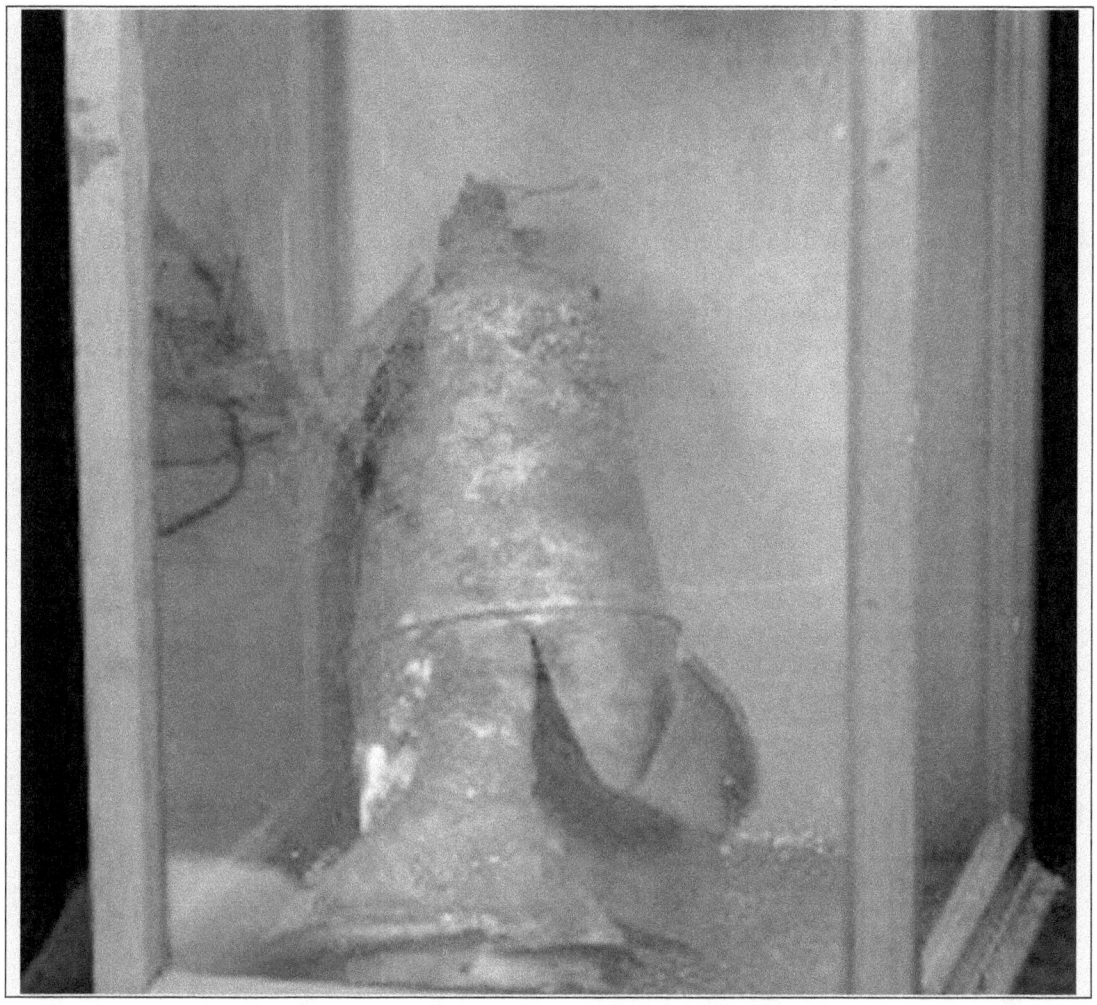

Figure 15. Part of the incendiary device that landed in the grounds of the Royal Infirmary, held in a glass display case. LHSA Object Collection, O26

(11) The eleventh bomb (high explosive) landed on a pavement area located outside the White Hart Hotel at 34 Grassmarket. Four persons were injured by the blast and shrapnel, one of whom died prior to the Police report being compiled. There was significant damage inflicted on the White Hart Hotel and windows were blown out on properties located at the northern end of Grassmarket and in the West Bow and West Port areas (NRS HH31/21/8 fols. 27-49).

(12) The twelfth bomb (high explosive) landed on castle rock at the South West corner of Edinburgh Castle. As well as damage to the rock, the blast blew in windows in Castle Terrace, Grindlay Street and Spittal Street (NRS HH31/21/8 fols. 27-49). (13) The thirteenth bomb (high explosive) landed on the roof of the County Hotel at 21 Lothian Road. There was significant damage to the building roof, the rear wall and interior – 18 rooms were damaged to various degrees. The gable end wall of an adjoining Hotel at 31 Lothian Road was destroyed and interior damage

inflicted – entrance doors and internal furniture in three rooms were destroyed. Casualties consisted of slight injury(s) to one person (NRS HH31/21/8 fols. 27-49).

(14) The fourteenth bomb (high explosive) landed in a valley that the Water of Leith coursed through, facing Coltbridge Gardens. This bomb destroyed a section of the embankment of the Water of Leith, a Dove Cot and blew out windows in eight dwellings in Coltbridge Gardens. The fifteenth and sixteenth bombs (both high explosive) also landed in the valley of the Water of Leith, (15) close to Mill Lade, blowing out windows of a stable and dwellings in Belford Park, and (16) landed in the vicinity of Donaldson's Hospital School blowing out 28 windows in the Hospital School Chapel and a number of windows in Belford Place, Belford Park, Douglas Crescent and Magdala Crescent (NRS HH31/21/8 fols. 27-49).

Figure 16. Bomb damage at 16 Marshall Street, Edinburgh. Reproduction of newspaper photograph of 9 February 1919.

(17) The seventeenth bomb (high explosive) struck a pavement area outside 16 Marshall Street, a dwelling on a tenement block. This bomb caused significant casualties – six persons killed and seven injured. The blast caused significant damage, the ground floor dwelling and staircase were destroyed, as were the cellars located underneath 16 Marshall Street, with significant window breakage in the general vicinity (NRS HH31/21/8 fols. 27-49).

(18) Three persons were injured when the eighteenth bomb (high explosive) landed at Haddow's Court in Nicolson Street. The blast of this bomb demolished a Sprit Merchants building and blew out windows of buildings in Haddow's Court, Nicolson Street and Simon Square. (19) A child was killed and two other persons injured when the nineteenth bomb (high explosive) struck a tenement dwelling, 69 St. Leonard's Hill, causing serious damage to the building and blowing out windows of other nearby buildings (NRS HH31/21/8 fols. 27-49).

Four bombs number 20-23 (one incendiary and three high explosive) landed on the southern part of King's Park. An incendiary (20) damaged a boundary wall and one of the high explosive bombs (21) damaged a roof of shops that adjoined King's Park and destroyed a total of 341 glass panes. There was no notable damage reported from the high explosive bombs (22 & 23). (24) The twenty fourth bomb (incendiary), the last bomb dropped on Edinburgh by *L.14*, landed within the grounds of Prestonfield House, Priestfield Road, with no notable damage reported (NRS HH31/21/8 fols. 27-49).

It is recorded in the Edinburgh City Police report that bomb number 17 fell around 00.40 hours on the morning of 3 April, but, as noted above, the same report states that the last of the 24 bombs dropped on Edinburgh was reported as falling at 00.25 hours (NRS HH31/21/8 fols. 27-49). If the 00.40 hours report is accurate for bomb number 17, it has to be considered that not only did this bomb fall some 15 minutes later than the last reported explosion, then other bombs may well have fallen after this time. The 00.40 time recorded for bomb number 17 may be erroneous, leaving the 00.25 hours as the recorded time for the last bomb explosion in Edinburgh on the morning of 3 April 1916.

List of casualties from the bombing raid on Edinburgh were as follows: (Bomb No.3) Mr. David Robertson (age 27), struck in abdomen by shrapnel and taken to the Royal Infirmary, but subsequently died of wounds. (Bomb No.7) Rose Fairley or Porteous, taken to the Royal Infirmary for treatment of injury to her right eye. Private Thomas Porteous (age 17), taken to Royal Infirmary for non-serious cuts and burns on head and face. William Porteous (age 13), suffered minor cuts on head. Jessie Hyndman or Halkett (age 25), taken to the Royal Infirmary and treated for cuts on head, face and left hand, and also treated for shock. William Halkett (age 30) Carter, slight cut on hand. Beatrice Pinkerton (age 2 months) treated for shock. All six were injured by the bomb that fell as at 183 Causewayside (NRS HH31/21/8 fols. 27-49).

(Bomb No.11) William Breakey (age 45) Carter was hit on the right of chest by shrapnel. He was taken to the Royal Infirmary, but subsequently died of his injury. Michael King (age 48) was taken to the Royal Infirmary and treated for serious injuries to the left leg and right shoulder. Catherine Cavennagh or O'Donnell (age 36) was treated for cuts on right forearm caused by broken glass. Robert Aitchison (age 44) minor injuries on throat, back, legs and forearm from broken glass. Isabella Tough or Ross (age 40) minor cut on the right cheek caused by broken glass. (Bomb No.17) In Marshall Street there were six persons killed – William Smith (age 15), John Smith (age 41), Henry George Rumble (age 17), David Thomas Graham (age 5), William Ewing (age 23) and Victor McFarlane. There were seven injured in Marshall Street – Margaret Hopetown or Bell (age 38), minor cut on head, Jessie Hossack or Dryden (age 42). minor cut on face, Janet Paton or Todd (age 70), minor cut on face, Eveline Todd (age 3) treated for shock at the Royal Infirmary, William Rumble (age 40), treated for a serious eye injury at the Royal Infirmary, James Smith (age 12), minor cut on leg and Private Thomas Donoghue (age 24), treated in the Royal Infirmary for serious abdomen wound and minor wounds on right leg and head (NRS HH31/21/8 fols. 27-49).

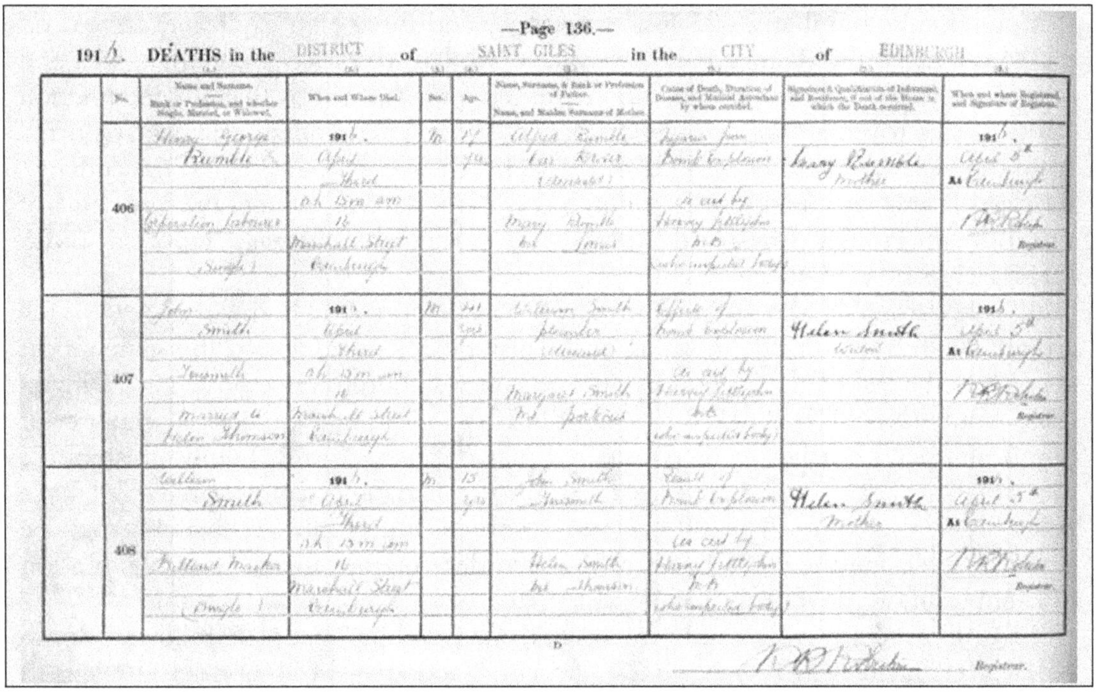

Figure 17. Form list detailing those killed by the bomb blast at 16 Marshall Street.

(Bomb No.18) Edward Arbuthnot (age 34), treated at the Royal Infirmary for a minor wound in the right leg, James Farquhar (age 74) minor injuries on right leg, Helen Mason or Brown (age 63), minor cut on chin. (Bomb No.19) A 4 year old infant, Cora Edmond Bell, was killed and Isabella Bertram or Bell (age 36), was treated at the Royal Infirmary for an injury to the right hand and shock (NRS HH31/21/8 fols. 27-49).

It is notable that most of the material damage resulting from the Zeppelin raid, in both Leith and Edinburgh, was caused by high explosive bombs. All of the fatalities and hospitalised casualties were the result of high explosive bombs, the incendiary devices proving, for the most part, to be ineffective in causing material damage or casualties. Experience of incendiary attacks in bomber offensives during the Second World War – 1939-1945 – would show that such weapons were most effective when employed in large numbers to saturate a target area, whereas the Zeppelin raids of World War 1 typically released small incendiary bombs one at a time. Furthermore, when such bombs impacted on a predominantly rock/stone/earth structure lacking combustible materials to provide fuel, they had limited ability to cause serious fires.

The Chief Constable of Leith's report, held in NRS HH31/21/8 fols.11-17, ended with a note about the behaviour of the civil populace, which he described as being 'on the whole very good' with no reports of 'pilfering' despite goods of many businesses being exposed (see Figure 18). Although not mentioned in the Edinburgh City Police report, there were no major incidents of looting reported in the city following the raid.

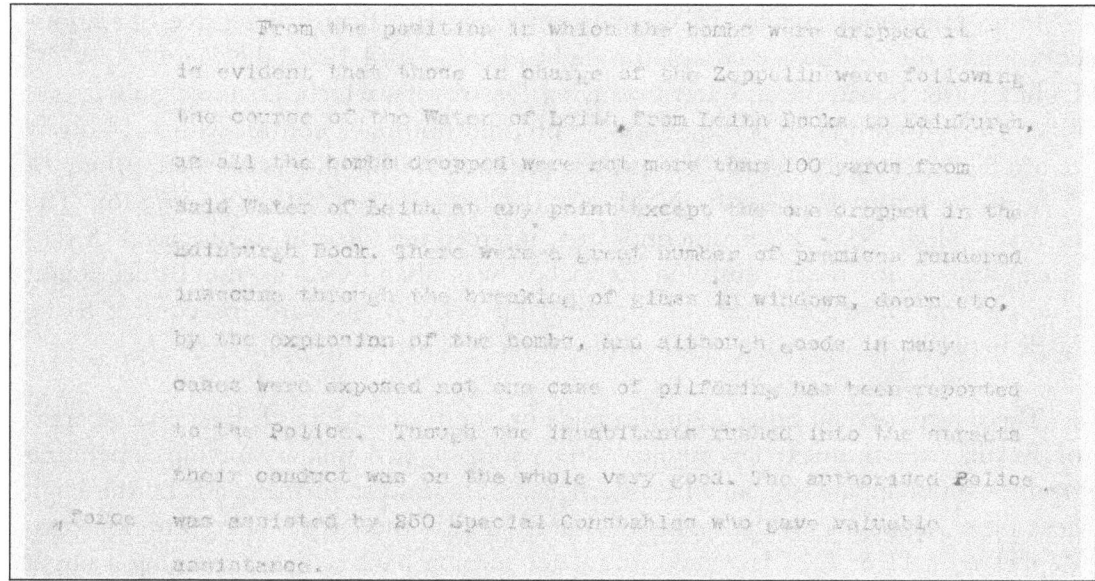

Figure 18. Extract from the Chief Constables of Leith's report on the Zeppelin raid of 2/3 April 1916. NRS HH31/21/8 fols.11-17

In reports drawn up after the raid there were statements that two Zeppelins dropped bombs on Edinburgh on the night of 2/3 April 1916. One of the most explicit reports drew on information provided by a Mrs. Lawson of Prestonfield Lodge whom claimed to have observed two airships at 00.15 hours on the morning of 3 April. One of these airships was reported as being flying 'a little higher than the other' over the King's Park area of Edinburgh, which was bombed (NRS HH31/21/8 fols. 27-49). As late as 2016, the 100th anniversary of the raid, the fallacy that two Zeppelins were over Edinburgh that night still persisted, despite overwhelming evidence from historical records that unequivocally proves that only a single Zeppelin, *L.14*, crossed the Scottish coast that night. One, reflective news story, dating from 2016, fallaciously states that Zeppelin *L.22*, commanded by Kapitanlieutenant Martin Dietrich, briefly passed over Edinburgh, before leaving and dropping its bombs in a field near Berwick-upon-Tweed. However, all reputable historical records clearly show that *L.22* was not within several hundred miles of Edinburgh that night, having bombed Cleethorpes just south of the Humber Estuary in England after it abandoned the attempt to reach Rosyth in the Forth Estuary (NSM XV, 1926, Air Raids 1916, III & Scheer, 1920).[19] The fact that only a single Zeppelin, *L.14*, was over Scotland on the night of 2/3 April 1916, is borne out by several Admiralty and War Office reports and Admiral Scheer, commander of the German High Sees Fleet, report on the attack, which merely mentions that the Firth of Forth had been reached by a Zeppelin 'for the first time' on the night of 2/3 April 1916 and that 'ships lying there and buildings along the Firth were attacked' (NSM XV, 1926, Air Raids 1916, III & Scheer, 1920).

---

[19] Cleethorpes is close to 300 miles South-eastward from Edinburgh

In an innocuous end to the German offensive and British defensive operations concerning the Zeppelin raids of the night of 2/3 April 1916, the Royal Navy 2nd Light Cruiser Squadron and accompanying Destroyers, which, as noted above, had sailed from Rosyth at 22.00 hours on 2 April, did not make contact with *L.*14 on its return flight across the North Sea and was ordered, at 07.00 hours on the morning of 3 April, to return to Rosyth (NSM XV, 1926 & Papers titled *X.*6767/16). The German High Seas Fleet intention of intercepting British light naval forces attempting to intercept returning Zeppelins was abandoned as the British Light Cruisers and Destroyers had not travelled far enough eastward for contact to be made between the opposing naval surface forces (NSM XV, 1926).

There were several other Zeppelin raids on the East and South East coastal areas of Britain over the next few nights. On 2/3 April, two military airships operating from Belgium apparently raided East Anglia.[20] There were further raids by the High Seas Fleet Zeppelins on the nights of 4 and 5 April, the targets being London (two Zeppelins, *L.*11 & *L.*17 launched, the latter turning back without reaching a target and the former dropping a few bombs over Norfolk before turning for home). A raid planned for three Zeppelins on the night of 4 April was cancelled due to inclement weather conditions, but three Zeppelins were launched on 5 April. *L.*13 turned back due to mechanical problems and *L.*11, tasked with attacking Rosyth in the Forth Estuary, plotted course for that local. However, strong winds pushed the Zeppelin southward, forcing the captain to abandon any hope of reaching the Forth. *L.*11 crossed the East coast of Yorkshire with the intention of bombing Sheffield. When on the approach to Hull, *L.*11 was engaged by anti-aircraft gunfire, which shook the airship, a shell exploding in close proximity. *L.*11 abandoned a plan to approach Sheffield from the direction of Hull and altered course out to sea with the intention of swinging round to attack Sheffield from the southward direction, but abandoned this idea after suffering a mechanical problem, which forced the decision to abandon the attack on Sheffield. Hartlepool was selected as the tertiary target as this was to windward, facilitating easier withdrawal from the target after the attack. *L.*11 fixed her position near Whitby, but was actually near Saltburn to the North of Whitby. Here she located suitable targets, 'smelting works and piers with steamers alongside' upon which she released all of her bombs, before heading out to sea for the return journey across the North Sea – only minor damage was caused to installations, with no casualties reported (NSM XV, 1926).

*L.*16 had observed *L.*11 come under artillery fire near Hull and was able to avoid this area by making landfall some distance north of Scarborough. She plotted course for Leeds, her intended target, which the crew thought had been reached around midnight, although the Zeppelin was in fact in the locality of Bishop Auckland, Durham. The bombs were released over what was thought to be 'factories, junctions and railway stations' at Leeds, but was in fact a Durham mining district where some cottages of mine workers were damaged with a single fatality (NSM XV, 1926). During the return journey one of the two Zeppelins was observed for a short period

---

[20] This raid is not acknowledged in the official German history

by the Royal Navy 10th Sloop Flotilla, which was sweeping a sea route, referred to as M Channel, southward from St Abbs Head (NSM XV, 1926). The operation on the night of 5 April marked the culmination of the Zeppelin raids of the New Moon period of late March and early April 1916, when conditions were most favourable.

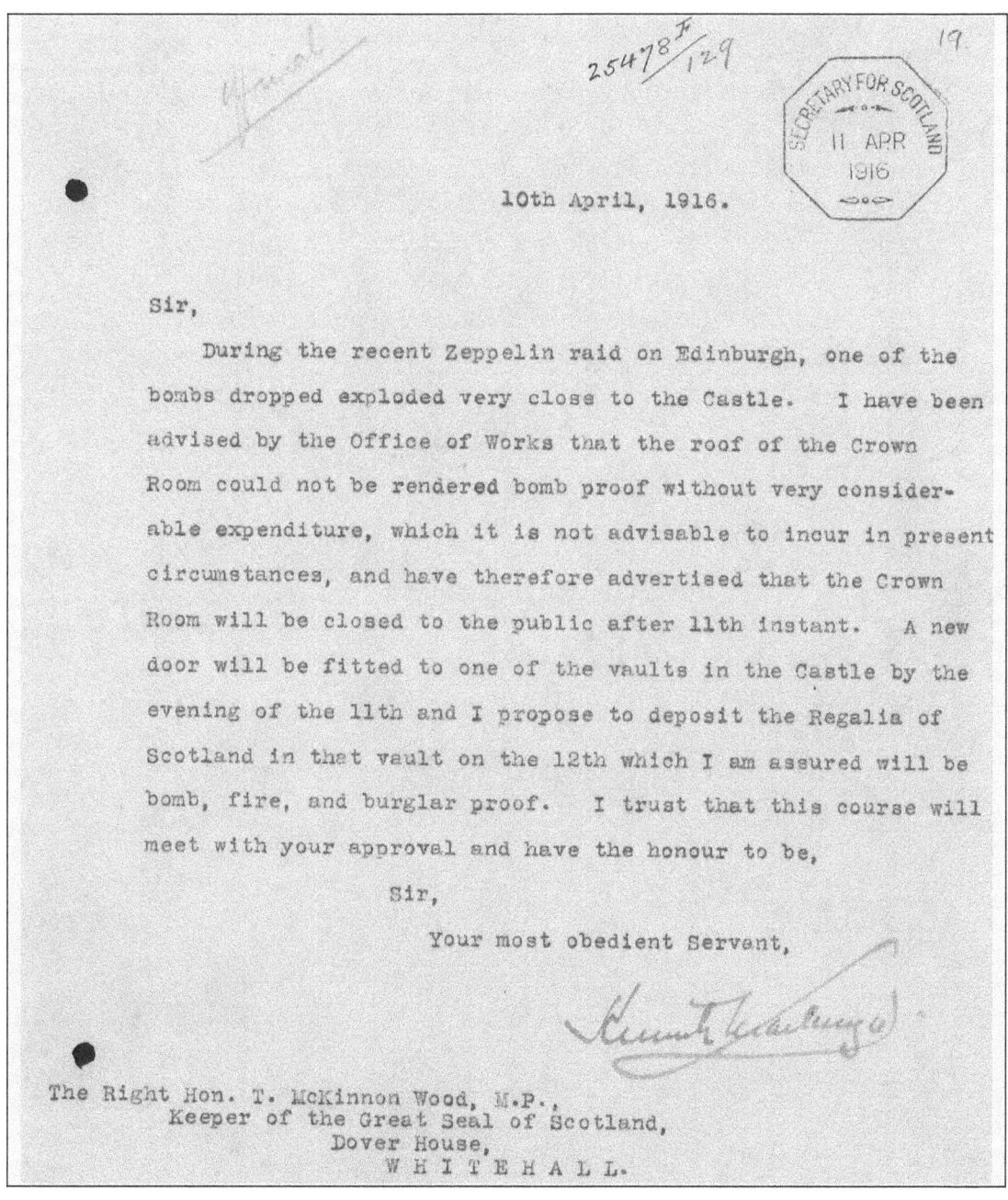

Figure 19. Letter, dated 16 April 1916, to the Keeper of the Great Seal of Scotland regarding a place of safety in which to store the Scottish Regalia, which, it was feared, was not adequately protected at in its place of residence at Edinburgh Castle.

C O P Y.

I hereby certify that I have attended Mrs. Smith off and on for the past five months. She has never recovered from the Zeppelin Raid on the 2nd. of April. She was confined in the early morning of that day, lost her nerve when she heard the bombs bursting round her, and had to be removed from the top flat of a four storey tenement to the basement passage of the common stair where she spent the night. In the morning she was removed to a nursing home. She did not make good recovery and has been nervous and sleepless since. She has no relations in the city or the country who could come to stay with her. It is doubtful if she would be able to stay in the house alone, and it certainly would add a strain that at present she is ill able to bear.

(SIGNED) W. Morrison Milne,
F.R.C.S.E.

August 22, 1916.

Figure 20. Letter, dated 22 August 1916, in support of a Ministry Service Appeal Tribunal.

> *Appeal*
>
> APPLICATION OF WILLIAM LAUDER:-
>
> Reference is respectfully made to my previous application made on 4th May 1916, under which I obtained exemption to 1st August 1916. Owing to being nursed on the breast, my child, born on 18th April, prematurely, is improving in health, but he requires the greatest care and attention. My wife is nursing him in order to give him every possible chance, but at a great sacrifice to herself owing to her weak physical condition. She is, and always has been, delicate, and since the Zeppelin Raid which brought on the birth of the child prematurely, her nerves have been completely shattered. She is unable to do her ordinary household work, and she has to get outside help. She suffers from Chronic Rheumatism and is at the present time being attended by the Doctor for this trouble. My wife's separation allowance, if I have to join the Army, would be £1.1/- per week, and I have received intimation from the Civil Liabilities Committee that I am to be allowed only £9.10/- per year extra. This makes the weekly allowance £1.4.7 which I submit is quite inadequate for the upkeep of my house and family, especially at the present value of £1. My rent, taxes and insurances amount to 8/- weekly, and I have to pay 3/- weekly for a washerwoman, which only leaves 13/7 to maintain my wife and two children in food, and to pay for coal and gas, clothing, medicines, and Doctor's Bills, and extras, which is totally insufficient apart from the state of my wife's health and the condition of my younger child. As compared with the above weekly sum of £1.4.7 my present earnings are £2.10/- weekly and it takes that sum to maintain us. On the ground of financial and domestic hardship I claim exemption.
>
> I wish to draw special attention to the inadequate grant made to me by the Civil Liabilities Committee.

Figure 21. Letter presented to the Ministry Service Appeal Tribunal for William Lauder.

As well as the immediate human and material cost, the Zeppelin raid on Edinburgh and Leith on 2/3 April 1916 had wider reaching social and cultural implications as shown in detailing letters presented to the Keeper of the Great Seal of Scotland (see Figure 19) and Ministry Service Appeal Tribunal on deferral of military service (see Figures 20 & 21). A letter to the Keeper of the Great Seal of Scotland regarding a place of safety in which to store the Scottish Regalia highlighted the fear that it was not adequately protected at its place of residence in Edinburgh Castle. This fear had been brought about due to one of the bombs of the Zeppelin raid on 2/3 April having landed in the vicinity of Edinburgh Castle. The letters to the Ministry Service Appeal Tribunal give a small indication of some of the hardships attributed to the raid. In the case of Figure 21 the appeals to the Military Service Appeals Tribunal appear to put forward the argument that the man being conscripted would leave the household without enough income to get by. An argument against such a case was that many households were financially worse off due to the needs of the war, including people being conscripted for military service.

COUNTY OF MIDLOTHIAN.

NOTICE TO THE PUBLIC
IN THE EVENT OF
AN AERIAL RAID.

THE CHIEF-CONSTABLE ISSUES THE FOLLOWING INSTRUCTIONS FOR THE GUIDANCE OF HOUSEHOLDERS IN THE COUNTY IN CASE OF AN AIR RAID:—

1. Immediately information is received that an Air Raid is imminent, the Gas—both Public and Private—will either be altogether cut off or be reduced to a minimum, and in those parts of the County where there is an Electric Installation, the Electric Light will be entirely cut off, and this should act as a warning that hostile aircraft is approaching or has begun an attack.

2. The Police at the same time will do their utmost to warn householders who use illuminants other than Gas or Electricity by informing them that an Air Raid is imminent, and this should be the signal for them to Extinguish all Inside Lights.

3. Householders using Gas are earnestly requested to extinguish what light remains, taking care to turn off the taps at the Gas Jets and Meter, to avoid danger in case of fire or of explosion or suffocation after the pressure is restored. Universal observance of this recommendation will produce the state of darkness which the Military Authorities consider so essential to public safety.

4. Householders, Shopkeepers, and others who are in the habit of keeping a small gas jet or jets burning overnight should discontinue the practice, as, with the gas reduced to a minimum in the event of an Air Raid, the light may go out, and on resumption of the pressure with open taps, the danger from suffocation and explosion is obvious.

5. The inhabitants are requested to remain Indoors during an Air Raid attack, keeping away from windows, and refraining from using lights of any kind. The danger of remaining outside is accentuated considerably by fragments of shells, &c., falling from our own defensive guns.

6. Unexploded Shells or Bombs should on no account be interfered with, as they may burst when moved, but immediately it can be done with safety the Police should be informed of their position. By Regulation 35B of the Defence of the Realm Regulations it is an offence for any person having found any Bomb or Projectile or any Fragment thereof, or any Document, Map, &c., which may have been discharged, dropped, &c., from any hostile aircraft not to forthwith communicate the fact to a Military Post or to a Police Constable in the neighbourhood.

7. No matches must be struck nor lights of any description shown immediately before or during an Air Raid. The Lighting Restrictions must be strictly observed by the inhabitants. Darkness and silence are essential to public safety.

S. W. DOUGLAS, Major,
Chief Constable.

County Rooms, Edinburgh,
24th March 1917.

Figure 22. Almost a year following the Zeppelin raid the Chief Constable of Edinburgh issued the above notice on what to do in the event of an air raid.

Figure 23. Port side on view of quasi-aircraft carrier/Light Battle Cruiser, HMS *Furious* working up in the Forth Estuary in 1917. WO

Figure 24. Port side-on view of *Furious* off May Island in the Forth Estuary. BO

In a twist of fate, on 19 July 1918 (just over twenty seven months) after the Zeppelin Raid on Edinburgh and Leith on the Forth Estuary, a force of warships sailed from Rosyth, Zeppelin *L*.14's original target, to launch an air raid on the Zeppelin sheds at Tondern Schleswig, with aircraft from the quasi-aircraft carrier/Light Battle Cruiser HMS *Furious*. *Furious* had worked up in the Firth of Forth after commissioning on 4 July 1917. The covering force for this historic carrier air attack was the five Revenge Class Battleships of the 1st Division, 1st Battle Squadron of the Grand Fleet and the 1st and 7th Light Cruiser Squadrons, all screened by Destroyers, with the entire force placed under the overall command of Admiral Sir Charles Madden, flying his flag in the 15 in gun Battleship HMS *Revenge* (Harkins, 2015).

Figure 25. Seven Sopwith 2F1 Camel bi-plane fighter aircraft on the forward flying-off deck of HMS *Furious* whist the vessel was sailing to the launch point for the air attack on the Zeppelin sheds at Tondern in July 1918. MOI

In conclusion it is shown by the evidence, the 2/3 April 1916 Zeppelin raid on Leith and Edinburgh was not an isolated or random attack, but part of a concerted Zeppelin effort against the British East coast in the New Moon period of early April 1916. The raid on Edinburgh involved only a single Zeppelin, L.14, and not two Zeppelins as is often stated in fallacious reflective news reports as late as the 100th anniversary of the raid. The other two Zeppelin that were active over the East Coast of Britain that night bombed targets further South on the East coast of England.

The raid was the only time that a Zeppelin bombed targets in Scotland during World War 1, but it was not intended to be an isolate incident. Rosyth had been a primary target for the High Seas Zeppelin Fleet, with no less than three separate missions, involving ten Zeppelin sorties, launched against it during the period 5 March to 5 April 1916. The sheer difficulty for the Zeppelins to reach such a northwesterly target as Rosyth is evinced by the fact that only a single Zeppelin was able to reach the Forth Estuary, Edinburgh and Leith being bombed due to the navigational problems in finding Rosyth.

In regard to the material damage and human cost of the raid, it is clear that the incendiary devices dropped from the Zeppelin proved to be ineffective – some landing on areas that had little to no combustible material. The high explosive bombs proved to be deadly effective, resulting in most of the material damage and all of the notable casualties in both Leith and Edinburgh.

The British defensive measures to target the Zeppelin proved to be ineffective, the single aircraft sent up to affect an interception being lost in a crash – the launch of an Avro 504C fighter aircraft from East Fortune airfield being the first air interception mission ever launched from Scotland – and the warships dispatched to intercept the airship on its return across the North Sea to Germany failing to make contact.

The raid had no detrimental effect on British naval operations emanating from Rosyth. As the war was in its last month's Rosyth would be the launch point for offensive operations against the Zeppelins at their base, the reverse of the situation that prevailed in April 1916.

GLOSSARY

BO	British Official
HMS	His Majesty's Ship
hp	Horsepower
III	Roman Numeral, number 3
LHSA	Lothian Health Services Archives
NRS	National Records Scotland
NSM	Naval Staff Monograph
RNAS	Royal Naval Air Service
The Great Seal of Scotland	Seala Mòr na h-Alba (Gaelic) Provisions monarchic authorisation for government documents
UK NA	United Kingdom National Archives
WO	War Office
XV	Roman Numeral, number 15
°	Degree(s)
~	Approximately equal to (can also be used to mean asymptotically equal)

BIBLIOGRAPHY

Admiralty Signals. 1200, 1210, 1212 of 5 March 1916, held in I.D.H.S records

Air Raids 1916, III, Official papers on air raids held in British archives

Airship Raids 1916, Official papers on Zeppelin air raids held in British archives

Chief Constable of Leith. (1916) *Report on the Zeppelin Air Raid, 2/3 April 1916*, National Records of Scotland, HH31/21/8 fols. 11-17

County of Midlothian. (1917) *Notice to the public in the event of an aerial raid,* issued by S.W. Douglas, Major, Chief-Constable, County Rooms, Edinburgh, National Records of Scotland, GD18-6182

Edinburgh City Archives (date unknown). Edinburgh Engineers map showing bomb impact areas

Hansard. (1916) *Vol 21 cc42-6642, transcript of Lord Oranmore & Browne speech in the Lords concerning Zeppelin raids on Britain with impunity*, 17 February 1916, Hansard Society

Harkins, H. (2015) *Light Battle Cruisers and the Second Battle of Heligoland Bight*, Centurion Publishing, United Kingdom

H.M. Government. (1915) Public Warning Poster, MEPO 2/1621, published under the authority of His (now Her) Majesty's Stationary Office

Jellicoe, Admiral, Viscount. (1919) *The Grand Fleet 1914-1916, Its Creation, Development and Work*, George H Doran Company, New York

LHSA (1916). *Details of Zeppelin raid effect on the Royal Infirmary*, Lothian Health Services Archives

McAusland, Peter. (1916) *Report on the Zeppelin raid on Edinburgh on the night of 2/3 April 1916*, Detective Inspector Criminal Investigation Department, Edinburgh City Police, National Records of Scotland, HH31/21/8 fols. 27-49

National Museums Scotland (2019). East Fortune History Sheet

Naval Staff Monographs (Historical), Fleet Issue. (1926) *Volume XV, Home Waters Part VI, from October 1915 to May 1916*, C.B. 917M. Naval Staff Training and Staff Duties Division

Official War Office papers. (1916) titled X.6767/1

Report by Captain Schulze. (1916) *L.11 Zeppelin raid of 4/5 March 1916*

Reports by Director of Air Services, H.S. 218

Right Hon. T. McKinnon Wood, M.P., Keeper of the Great Seal of Scotland. (1916) Letter to the Secretary for Scotland regarding a place of safety in which to store the Scottish Regalia, 10 April 1916

Royal Infirmary Hospital. (1916) *Extract from the General Register of patients at the Royal Infirmary, describing injuries sustained in the Zeppelin raid*, LHB1/126/61

Sheer. (1920) *Germany's High Seas Fleet in the World War*, Cassell and Company Ltd, London, New York, Toronto and Melbourne

W. Morrison Milne, F.R.C.S.E. (1916) Letter of evidence presented to the Ministry Service Appeal Tribunal in support of Peter Smith's appeal, 22 August 1916

Unidentified author. (1916) Letter presented to the Ministry Service Appeal Tribunal for William Lauder

Form list of fatalities at 16 Marshall Street caused by the Zeppelin raid on 2/3 April 1916, D1916_685_04_0136Z

Hand written list of persons killed at No's 16 and 33 Marshall Street

Photograph showing damage at Edwin Place, Porter Street, Hull, from Zeppelin raid, AIR 1-569-16-15-142

Photograph of incendiary bomb remnants, Lothian Health Services Archives object collection, O26

Photograph of incendiary bomb remains in the grounds of the Royal Infirmary, 1916, (P/PL1/E/021)

Photograph of damage to buildings in the area of the Royal Infirmary, 3 April 1916 (P/PL1/E/208)

The National Archives, Zeppelin Raids

Transcript of Edinburgh Fire Brigade report on the Zeppelin raid of 2/3 April 1916

ABOUT THE AUTHOR

Hugh Harkins FRAS is a historian and author with an extensive research/study background in aeronautic, astronautic, astro/geophysics, nautical and the wider scientific, technical and historical fields. He is also involved in research in the field of Scottish history, which formed significant elements of dual undergraduate degrees. Hugh has published in excess of sixty books, non-fiction and fiction, writing under his given name as well as utilising several pseudonyms. He has also written for several international magazines, whilst his work has been used as reference for many other projects, ranging from the aviation industry, international news corporations and film media to encyclopaedias, museum exhibits and the computer gaming industry. Hugh is a member of the Institute of Physics and is an elected Fellow of the Royal Astronomical Society. He currently resides in his native Scotland. Other titles by the author include:

Raid on the Forth - The First German Air Raid on Great Britain in World War II
The Battle of Kilsyth, 15 August 1645 - Montrose Baillie and The Keys to Scotland
Light Battle Cruisers and the Second Battle of Heligoland Bight
Into The Cauldron - The Lancaster MK.I Daylight Raid on Augsburg
Hurricane IIB Combat Log - 151 Wing RAF, North Russia 1941
RAF Meteor Jet Fighters in World War II, an Operational Log
Typhoon IA/B Combat Log - Operation Jubilee, August 1942
Defiant MK.I Combat Log - Fighter Command, May-September 1940
Blenheim MK.IF Combat Log - Fighter Command Day Fighter Sweeps/Night Interceptions, September 1939 - June 1940
Fortress MK.I Combat Log - Bomber Command High Altitude Bombing Operations, July-September1941
Soviet Mixed Power Experimental Fighter Aircraft – Piston-Liquid Propellant Rocket Engine/Piston-Ramjet/Piston-Pulsejet & Piston-Compressor Jet Engine Designs of the 1940's
Russia's Coastal Missile Shield - Bal-E & Bastion Mobile Coastal Cruise Missile Complexes
Iskander - Mobile Tactical Aero-Ballistic/Cruise Missile Complex
Orbital/Fractional Orbit Bombardment System - The Soviet Globalnaya Raketa
Counter-Space Defence Co-Orbital Satellite Fighter
Russia's Strategic Missile Carrier/Bomber Roadmap 2018-2040 – PAK DA, Tu-160M2, Tu-95MSM & Tu-22M3M
Sukhoi T-50/PAK FA - Russia's 5th Generation 'Stealth' Fighter
Sukhoi Su-35S 'Flanker' E - Russia's 4++ Generation Super-Manoeuvrability Fighter
Sukhoi Su-30MKK/MK2/M2 - Russo Kitashiy Striker from Amur
MiG-35/D 'Fulcrum' F – Towards the Fifth Generation
Air War over Syria, Tu-160, Tu-95MS & Tu-22M3 - Cruise Missile and Bombing Strikes on Syria, November 2015-February 2016
Sukhoi Su-27SM(3)/SKM
Russian/Soviet Aircraft Carrier & Carrier Aviation Design & Evolution Volume 1 - Seaplane Carriers, Project 71/72, Graf Zeppelin, Project 1123 ASW Cruiser & Project 1143-1143.4 Heavy Aircraft Carrying Cruiser
Light Battle Cruisers and the Second Battle of Heligoland Bight
British Battlecruisers of World War 1 - Operational Log, July 1914-June 1915
Eurofighter Typhoon - Storm over Europe
North American F-108 Rapier - Mach 3 Interceptor
Convair YB-60 - Fort Worth Overcast
Boeing X-36 Tailless Agility Flight Research Aircraft
X-32 - The Boeing Joint Strike Fighter

www.ingramcontent.com/pod-product-compliance
Lightning Source LLC
Chambersburg PA
CBHW081509040426
42446CB00017B/3442